A View From a Hill

AF353811

Aidan Hill

BookLeaf
Publishing

A View From a Hill © 2022 Aidan Hill

All rights reserved.

No part of this publication may be reproduced, stored in a retrieval system, or transmitted, in any form or by any means, electronic, mechanical, photocopying, recording or otherwise, without the prior written permission of the presenters.

Aidan Hill asserts the moral right to be identified as author of this work.

Presentation by *BookLeaf Publishing*

Web: www.bookleafpub.com

E-mail: info@bookleafpub.com

ISBN: 9789357448727

First edition 2022

DEDICATION

For my encouraging mother

and my inspiring father

Shepherd

Christ, a good shepherd,
leads us, guides us, to better
pastures and waters.

Nugget

A crispy nugget,
when dipped in sauce, so tasty.
Oh crap! I dropped it...

A Crack

More annoying than the thorn in my side,
is your crack on my butt, Chair.

Pepsi

I taste the flat, day old, lukewarm Pepsi that I
left out last night,
but love too much to throw away like long
forgotten garbage.
"They'll be the death of ya" mom said, and yes,
soon I'll see the light,
but the sweetness and fizzle on the tongue leads
me to stock the fridge.

Snowboarding

The snowboard glides.
I slip, it slides.
The wind is rushing past;
this thrill is a blast.
Fast.
I lean into the curve,
there is no one to observe.
I can almost fly,
My snowboard and I.

This is just to say

I took off
in my truck
to go to
college.

I know
that you
wanted me
near.

Forgive me,
but I go
to learn
and grow.

Rain

The silencing rain,
Crashed down on my umbrella.
What a pleasant day.

Oreos

Oreos, so good.
Whole milk to dunk in... How long?
Whoops, it's too soggy.

Warm

The blanket's so warm.
Blaring alarms broke through dreams.
Five more minutes please.

Reading

On a silent night
the fire popped and crackled.
Good times with my book.

Stone

Slipping on my shoe.
Ouch! An unpleasant surprise...
I found a small stone.

Colors

Autumn's falling leaves,
came to rest on the side-walk,
painting all the streets.

Chaucer's College Hipster

The Hipster has but one dream
To never be too mainstream
On his face lies black-rimmed glasses
Purely for his fashion senses
A plaid scarf is around his neck,
Even though it's hot as heck
He burnt his tongue, while on a stool
He drank coffee before it was cool!
His trusty typewriter in one hand,
Which he uses for fiction, and
For his classes at the university,
He writes papers of much diversity.
He acts like he knows the best,
And he'll tell you, without a jest.
Not many people like him at first,
But he'll be with you through the worst.

Invincible River of
Boredom

Every morning I think, "quarantine sucks".
Minutes, hours, and days flow by
in the invincible river of boredom. The clocks
say so at least... I can only watch the time fly.
I have opened and closed the fridge door.
I've sat and laid on every cushion of the couch
I wonder if I should try laying on the floor.
What more could I do? I've already grown a
slouch!
I've played Minecraft, read four books,
and even write sometimes, but my feet
are restless... Should I sort the forks?
Ideas float down the river like a strange fleet.
I tried them out as if the ideas were my own.
One by one I think, "this is kind of dumb."
No matter what I do, I can't slow down
the Invincible river of boredom.

My Mind

The complexities, the perplexities.
Pebbles of ponderings thrown about.
Faces, memories, Images;
fleeting moments telling parts of a story.

The rocky ground forms a path,
where holes, bumps, and bushes lay
as obstacles in the path of time.

Brambles of relations intertwined
to create bonds which
last forever, if watered
with love.

The tree of family, in its shade
a quiet comfortable place to stop
and think about nothing that means everything.

Pools of emotion, swelling,
flooding my reservoir.
The joy shimmering on top like reflected stars.
The darkness pushed down deep in the murky
depths.

The sky above filled with hopes,

dreams,
and possibilities.

A maze of experiences,
the labyrinth of my mind.

Prompt: Missing someone

Pain dulled my senses.
The realization like a great weight
muted the world to whispers,
Time, that had sped through the laughing years,
now moved slowly as it blurred past unnoticed.

Sorrow filled my bones.
The procession, like black ants in a line,
trudged their way to the cemetery.
The earth opened and received her casket.
My heart, once open, closed like the earth

Loneliness stirred my mind.
Memories, like a guarded treasure,
crowded through the empty house,
filled the sleepless nights.
    She is everywhere,
    stirring the air.
The wind through the trees her sigh.

Unprofitable Servant

What am I, but an unprofitable servant?
I see thy hand and hear thy call to grab hold,
but my heavy heart often shuns the hand you
lent.
My Lord I can't grab on, my soul has been sold.
Tears blur my vision, but I feel thy hand, left
untaken,
on my back. "Don't worry, I am the one who
judges."
His words shook the dark and I know I am not
forsaken.
From the depths of Hell, He bought the
passages.

What am I, but an unprofitable servant?
Have I done my Master any good worth gold?
Two years? Nothing compared to His life spent.
Our contract, signed and sealed before the
world,
easily left forgotten, blemished and broken.
But still, He, My Lord, forgives the charges.
Weaknesses, temptations, He leaves unspoken.

To the path of redemption, He built the bridges.

What am I, but an unprofitable servant?
I hear of stranger's good deeds, but I'm not as
bold.
I see someone's need, but at times fear keeps me
silent.
Failures in trials, in kindness, and in life often
unfold
but my Lord, in mercy, says I am forgiven.
The efforts I've given aren't enough, but He
trims the edges.
Under the Master's wings, I am not mistaken.
From weakness to strength, He set the stages.

What am I, but an unprofitable servant?
Once, I was living in the dark and in the cold,
But now, with my Master's light, my faith is
ardent.
My master is the Lord, with Him I am bold.
Grace, love, and peace fill His words, unshaken.
For Him I crossed the highest mountain ledges,
sharing the white fruits that I have once
partaken.
For at the top of the Heavens, He prepared our
lodges.

The Meaning of Language

What is the meaning of language?
Well, to me the answer is pretty simple,
It's used to speak and not sound like garbage.
Communication is a must, if we live with
people.

And yet if it is so simple, why is it so difficult?
I try to give an explanation of my P.O.V.,
But receive angry or confused looks—was that
my fault?
Sometimes I'm not very clear, so perhaps it
could be.

My mind often drifts across to other dimensions
And loses track of the Universe of the
Discourse,
Maybe it can also forget the contexts of
conversations,
And I say things off-topic, leaving me feeling a
little remorse.

Ok, so language isn't simple, as it is in my own
thoughts.
If only we spoke to each other in propositions,
Free from context and is either true or false!
But life isn't easy, despite my many petitions.

And so we must deal with predicates and their
degrees,
Seriously, it's so senseless to have that many
senses...
And try to work out all of the different
ambiguities,
Be it structural, lexical, or pragmatic, from those
sentences.

Don't get me started on the Logical
Connectives!
They aren't predicates, yet the Truth Value is
still affected.
The entire meaning can change depending on the
Notations.
Things can be equivalent, entailed, inferred, or
implied.

And to make matters worse there are all of the
Fallacies
Most are unintentional mistakes in people's
logical thinking,

But some are used to manipulate the mental
faculties
Or to distract you from the argument, like with a
Red Herring.

It is even harder still when people flout the
Maxims,
The unexpected shift in the topic of the
utterance,
Although most people would just call that
Sarcasm,
We know that they've broken Grice's rule of
Relevance.

Language can be confusing and hard to
understand,
But I just have to admit that despite my various
troubles
The complexity of it all creates wonderful
diversity across the land.
And that more than makes up the price, far more
than double.

Language is an amazing tool that can bring
people together,
Or it can be a tool that can be used to drive
people away.
The choice is ours, like with any tool, to do
whichever.

I'm not a great talker, but I'll try my best to
brighten someone's day.

23

Early Wednesday Morning

In the early Wednesday morning,
with the sun still hours away,
all the roommates were sleeping,
and the blankets were warm where I lay.
Far too warm, sweat dripped off me,
and a burning fever left my mind confused.
Hacking coughs made my breath raspy.
I'm sorry friends, was your sleep disturbed?
Why isn't the medicine working?
I have too much to do tomorrow.
Laying back, I stare up at the ceiling,
praying that I'll recover enough to go.
I try to sigh but I just get another fit.
My eyes feel like lead and start to close,
but in the window I see the world's now lit.
It can't be helped, that's how life goes.

They Say

They say
It's the Devil.
It's not,
It's me.
My own mind
A traitor.
Maybe it
Was him
Who started
The process,
But now...
"I'm unworthy"
"I'm worthless"
"I'm disgusting"
"I'm unlovable"
My thoughts,
Perpetual.
I know,
In theory,
I'm wrong.
My friends
And family
Tell me,
"You're still worthy"
"You're divine"

"You're amazing"
"You're loved."
These words,
My thoughts
At war.
The light
And dark
At war.
Redemption,
Temptation
At war.
Oh Lord...
Help me.

Good Health and Blessings

When you're alone in cold and dark settings,
the Lord's strength is more than enough, so
I'll pray for your good health and blessings.

The light on the hill can help you find your
bearings
and provide relief against your one true foe,
when you're alone in cold and dark settings.

Of course, not everyone shares these same
feelings,
and despise when people say, since long ago,
"I'll pray for your good health and blessings."

But having faith in a heavenly Father brings
a hopeful new perspective that helps you grow
when you're alone in cold and dark settings.

I wish I could do more, despite all of my
failings,
but I'll call the one who is able to sooth your
woe,

I'll pray for your good health and blessings.

I love and care for you, with all of my heart's
beatings.
And so, at the end of the day, I hope that you
know,
when you're alone in cold and dark settings,
I'll pray for your good health and blessings.

www.ingramcontent.com/pod-product-compliance
Lightning Source LLC
LaVergne TN
LVHW021338200726
843509LV00014B/2571